Zaner-Bloser
Handwriting

Author

Clinton S. Hackney, Ed.D.

Reviewers

Julie Althide, Teacher, Hazelwood School District, St. Louis, Missouri

Becky Brashears, Teacher, Gocio Elementary, Sarasota, Florida

Douglas Dewey, Teacher, National Heritage Academies, Grand Rapids, Michigan

Jennifer B. Dutcher, Teacher, Elk Grove School District, Sacramento, California

Gita Farbman, Teacher, School District of Philadelphia, Philadelphia, Pennsylvania

Susan Ford, Teacher, St. Ann's School, Charlotte, North Carolina

Brenda Forehand, Teacher, David Lipscomb Middle School, Nashville, Tennessee

Sharon Hall, Teacher, USD 443, Dodge City, Kansas

Sr. James Madeline, Teacher, St. Anthony School, Allston, Massachusetts

Lori A. Martin, Teacher, Chicago Public Schools, Chicago, Illinois

Vikki F. McCurdy, Teacher, Mustang School District, Oklahoma City, Oklahoma

Melissa Neary Morgan, Reading Specialist, Fairfax County Public Schools, Fairfax, Virginia

Sue Postlewait, Literacy Resource Consultant, Marshall County Schools, Moundsville, West Virginia

Gloria C. Rivera, Principal, Edinburg CISO, Edinburg, Texas

Rebecca Rollefson, Teacher, Ericsson Community School, Minneapolis, Minnesota

Susan Samsa, Teacher, Dover City Schools, Dover, Ohio

Zelda J. Smith, Instructional Specialist, New Orleans Public Schools, New Orleans, Louisiana

Occupational Therapy Consultant: Maureen E. King, O.T.R.

Credits

Art: Diane Blasius: 4, 60, 62, 64, 66, 67, 100, 102, 104, 106, 107; Ruth Flanigan: 6, 7; John Hovell: 30, 31, 50, 51, 68, 69, 90, 91, 118; Tom Leonard: 3, 32, 34, 36, 38, 39, 70, 72, 76, 78; Sharron O'Neil: 4, 22, 23, 24, 25, 26, 27, 28, 29, 112, 113; Diane Paterson: 47; Nicole Rutten: 40, 42, 44, 46; Andy San Diego: 3, 8, 9, 14, 16, 18, 19, 20, 74, 78, 80, 82, 84, 86, 88, 89, 110, 111, 114, 115; John Wallner: 48, 52, 54, 56, 58, 59, 92, 94, 96, 98, 99

Photos: George C. Anderson Photography, Inc.: 5, 10, 11, 12, 13

Development: Kirchoff/Wohlberg, Inc., in collaboration with Zaner-Bloser Educational Publishers

ISBN 0-7367-1210-0   10 11 12   159   20 19 18 17 16 15

Contents

Writing Letters and Words

Shape

Size

Spacing

Slant

Using What You've Learned

Show what else you can write here. Draw a picture about your writing.

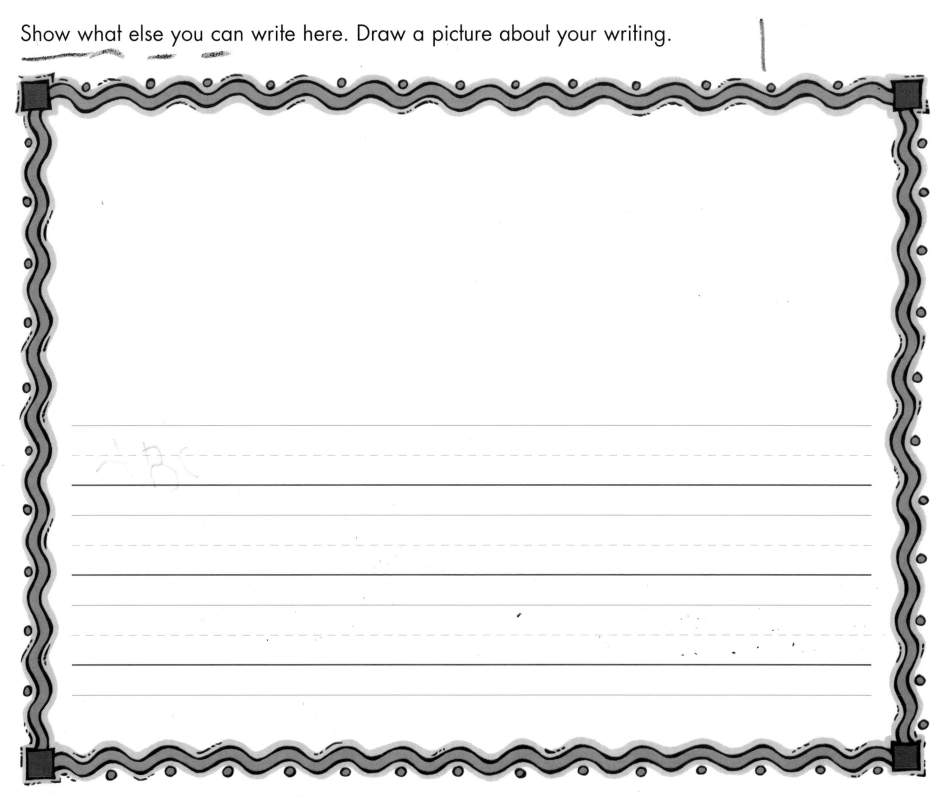

Letters and Numerals

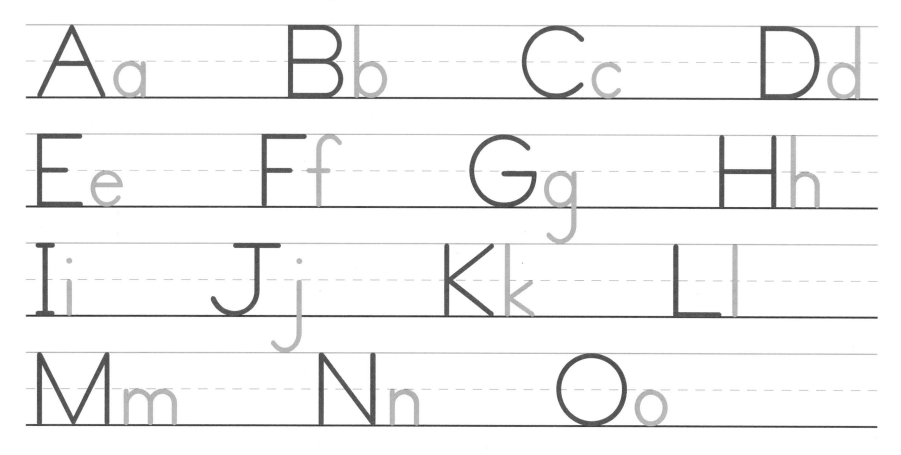

Trace the uppercase letter that begins your name.
Trace the lowercase letters in your name.

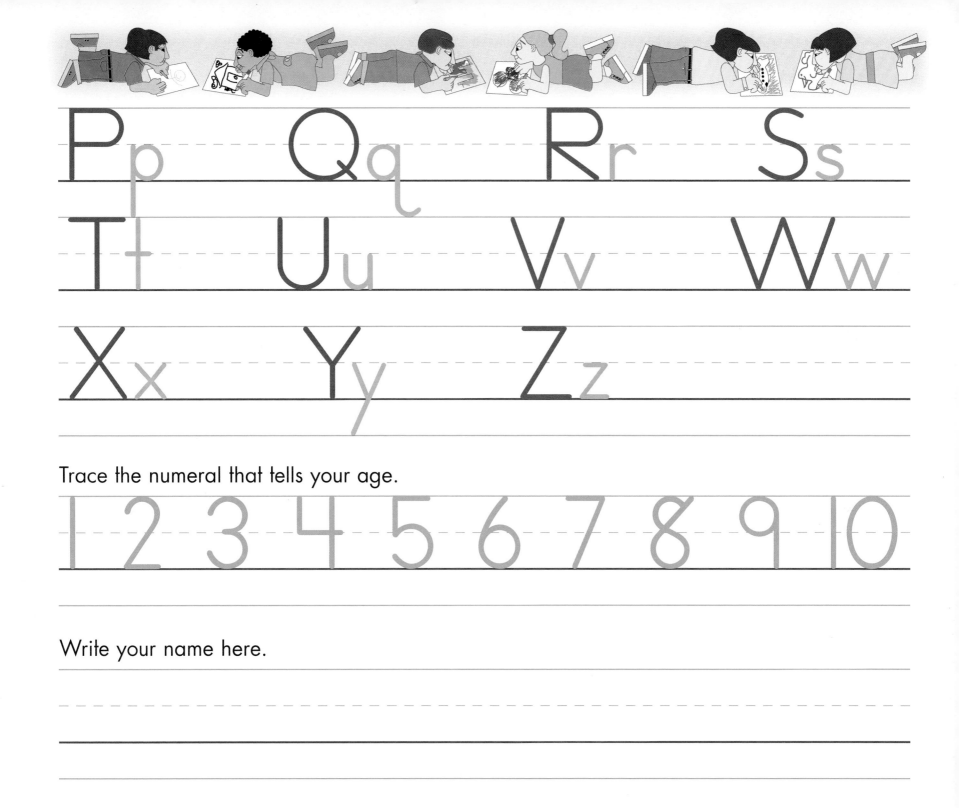

P p Q q R r S s

T t U u V v W w

X x Y y Z z

Trace the numeral that tells your age.

1 2 3 4 5 6 7 8 9 10

Write your name here.

If you write with your left hand. . .

Sit like this.

Sit comfortably. Lean forward a little.
Keep your feet flat on the floor.

Place the paper like this.

Slant the paper as shown in the picture.

Rest both arms on the desk. Use your right hand to move the paper as you write.

Pull the pencil toward your left elbow when you write.

Hold the pencil like this.

Hold the pencil with your thumb and first two fingers.

Do not squeeze the pencil when you write.

If you write with your right hand. . .

Sit like this.

Sit comfortably. Lean forward a little.
Keep your feet flat on the floor.

Place the paper like this.

Place the paper straight in front of you.

Rest both arms on the desk. Use your left hand to move the paper as you write.

Pull the pencil toward the middle of your body when you write.

Hold the pencil like this.

Hold the pencil with your thumb and first two fingers.

Do not squeeze the pencil when you write.

Your Book

Models and Guidelines

There are writing models in your book.
The models are on guidelines.

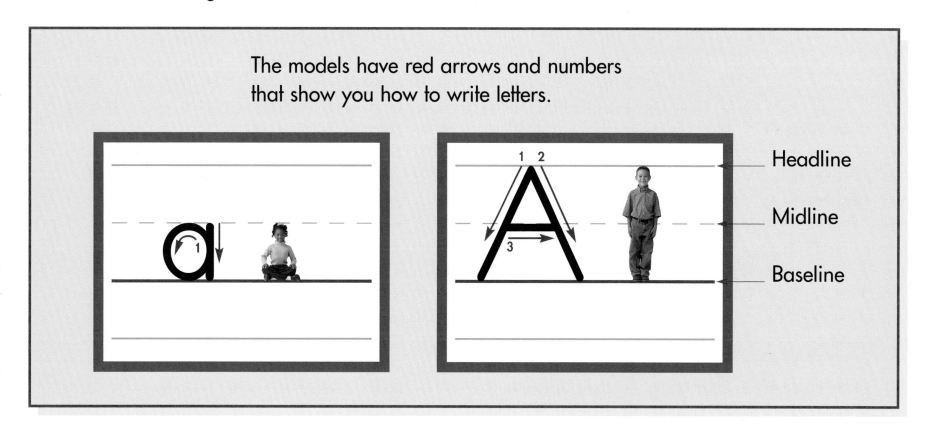

The models have red arrows and numbers
that show you how to write letters.

Headline

Midline

Baseline

Start at the green dot when you trace and write.

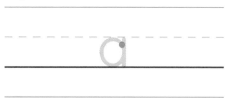

Stop and Check

You will see stop and check signs in your book when you finish a line of writing. When you see this sign, stop and circle the best letter you wrote on that line.

Circle the best letter on this line.

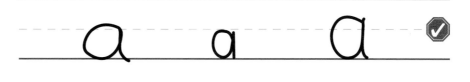

Keys to Legibility

There are four kinds of keys in your book.
The words on the keys are **Shape, Size, Spacing,** and **Slant**.
Good writers think about these things when they write.

The keys will help you make sure your writing is legible.
Legible means easy to read.

13

Basic Strokes
Vertical Lines

Some letters and numerals have lines that are straight up and down.

Trace the straight up and down lines in these letters and numerals.

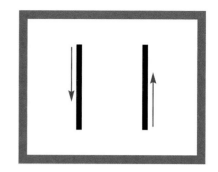

H D E t b i 9 4

Start at the green dot. ●
Trace the vertical lines.

Start at the green dot. •
Trace and write. Pull down straight.

Trace and write. Push up straight.

Horizontal Lines

Some letters and numerals have slide lines.

Trace the slide lines in these letters and numerals.

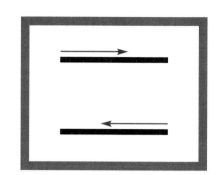

F G B z f e 5 7

Start at the green dot. •
Trace the slide lines.

Start at the green dot. •
Trace and write. Slide right.

Trace and write. Slide left.

Backward Circle Lines

Some letters and numerals have backward circle lines.

Trace the backward circle lines in these letters and numerals.

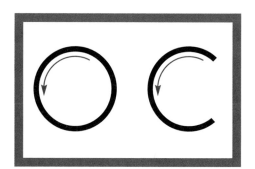

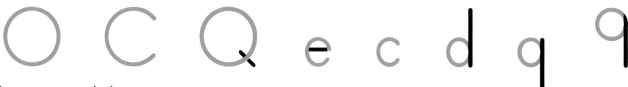

Start at the green dot. •
Trace the backward circle lines.

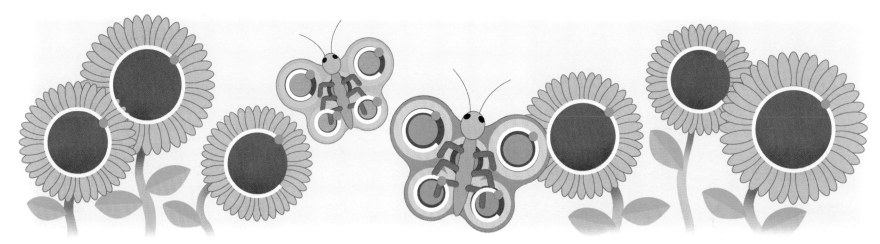

Trace and write. Circle back.

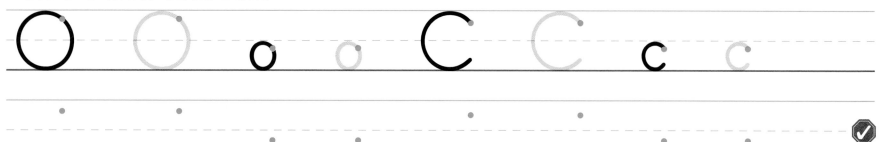

Forward Circle Lines

Some letters and numerals have forward circle lines.

Trace the forward circle lines in these letters and numerals.

R P D b 5 3

Start at the green dot. •
Trace the forward circle lines.

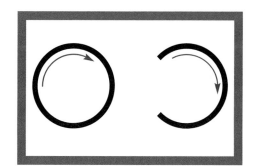

Trace and write. Circle forward.

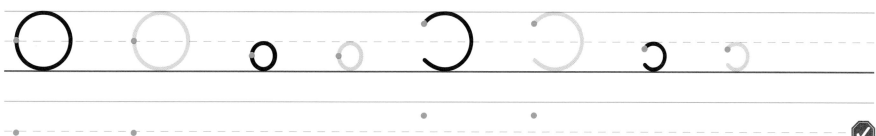

Basic Strokes
Slant Lines

Some letters and numerals have slant lines.

Trace the slant lines in these letters and numerals.

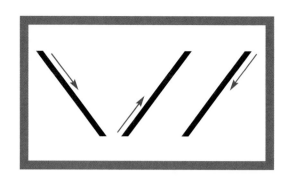

A N Q y w z 2 7

Start at the green dot. •
Trace the slant lines.

Start at the green dot. •
Trace and write. Slant right.

Trace and write. Slant left.

Trace and write. Slant up.

Writing Numerals

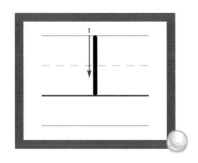  

Trace and write.

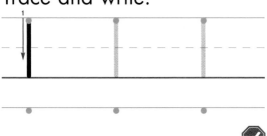 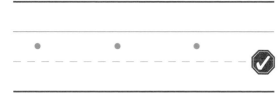 

Stroke descriptions to guide numeral formation at home:

1   Pull down straight.

2   Curve forward; slant left.
Slide right.

3   Curve forward.
Curve forward.

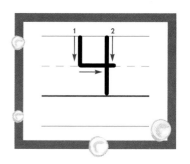

Trace and write.

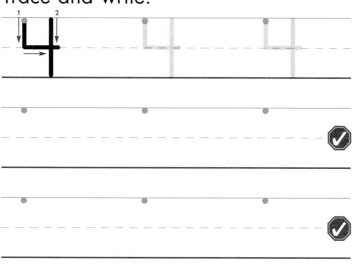

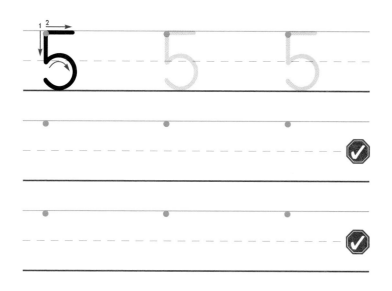

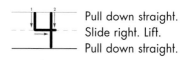 Pull down straight.
Slide right. Lift.
Pull down straight.

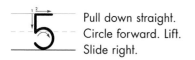 Pull down straight.
Circle forward. Lift.
Slide right.

23

Trace and write.

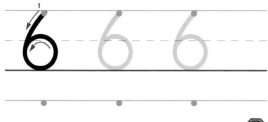
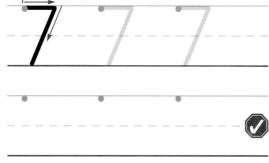
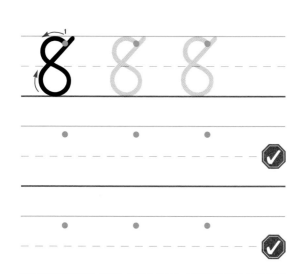

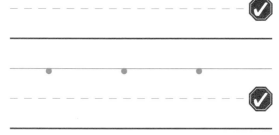
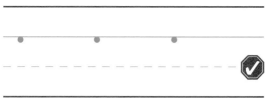

Stroke descriptions to guide numeral formation at home:

6   Curve down. Curve up and around.

7   Slide right. Slant left.

8   Curve back; curve forward. Slant up.

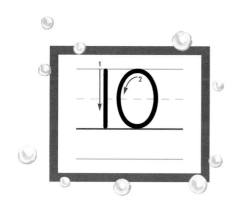

Trace and write.

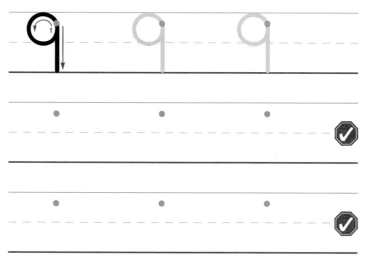

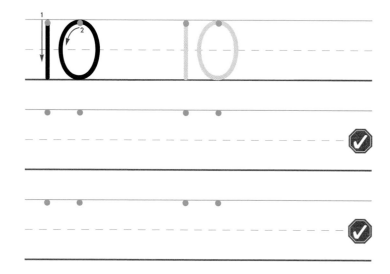

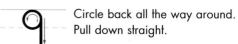 Circle back all the way around.
Pull down straight.

 Pull down straight. Lift.
Curve down; curve up.

Practice

Write **1 – 5**.

1   2   3   4   5

On Your Own

Write a numeral. Draw a picture to show how many.

Write **6 – 10**.

6   7   8   9   10

On Your Own

Write a numeral. Draw a picture to show how many.

Application

Write the number sentences.

1 + 2 = 3

+ =

5 + 1 = 6

+ =

7 + 2 = 9

+ =

4 + 4 = 8

+ =

Write the number sentences.

$$5 - 1 = 4$$

$$\_\_ - \_\_ = \_\_$$

$$8 - 7 = 1$$

$$\_\_ - \_\_ = \_\_$$

$$9 - 6 = 3$$

$$\_\_ - \_\_ = \_\_$$

$$10 - 2 = 8$$

$$\_\_ - \_\_ = \_\_$$

29

Keys to Legibility

Make your writing easy to read.
Look at the shape of each letter.

Shape

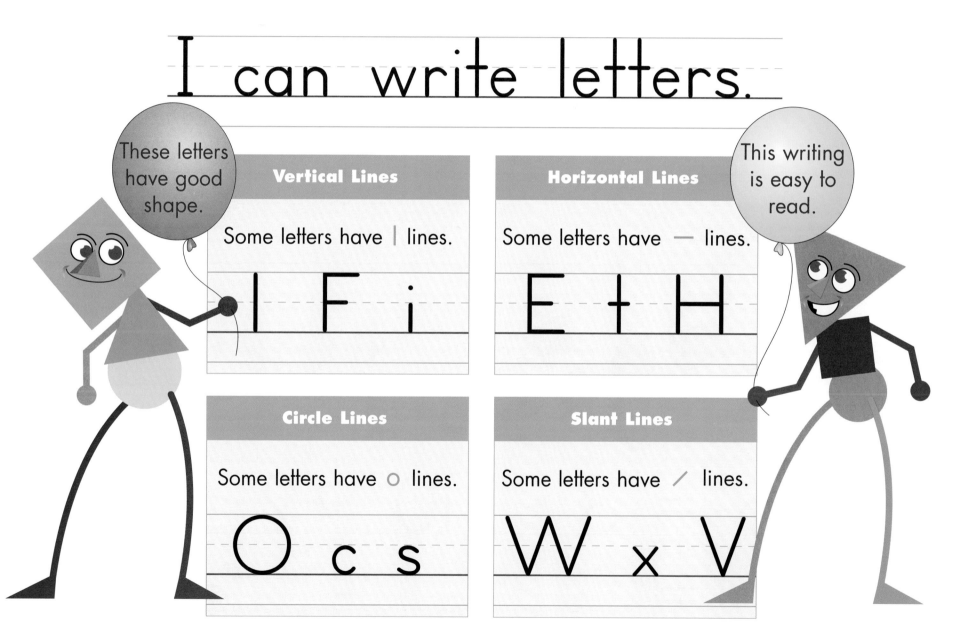

I can write letters.

These letters have good shape.

This writing is easy to read.

Vertical Lines

Some letters have | lines.

I F i

Horizontal Lines

Some letters have — lines.

E t H

Circle Lines

Some letters have ○ lines.

O c s

Slant Lines

Some letters have / lines.

W x V

Trace the | lines in these letters.

I T P D R h p r

Trace the — lines in these letters.

E F L H G A e f

Trace the ○ lines in these letters.

O C S B c s o q

Trace the ╱ ╲ lines in these letters.

Q X K M v w x k

Trace and write.

Trace and write.

✓

✓

✓

✓

leaf   like

Lola   Len

Stroke descriptions to guide letter formation at home:

Pull down straight.

Pull down straight.
Slide right.

Write the words.

lemon   lake   live   love

Write the sentence.

Look at my letters.

Write words to finish the sentence.

My letters are

Shape

Circle your best letter
that has a l line.

Trace and write.

Trace and write.

insect   lit

Ivan   Ida

School to Home

Stroke descriptions to guide letter formation at home:

Pull down straight. Lift. Dot.

Pull down straight. Lift.
Slide right. Lift. Slide right.

Write the words.

inch   ill   into   it

Write the sentence.

I like to write my name.

On Your Own Write words to finish the sentence.

I really like

Shape

Circle your best letter that has a **l** line.

Trace and write.

Trace and write.

turtle talk

Tate Tara

Stroke descriptions to guide letter formation at home:
Pull down straight. Lift. Slide right.

Pull down straight. Lift. Slide right.

School to Home

Write the words.

toy   tub   tell   take

Write the sentence.

This is my toy train.

On Your Own Write words to finish the sentence.

Toy trains are

Shape

Circle your best letter
that has a — line.

Practice

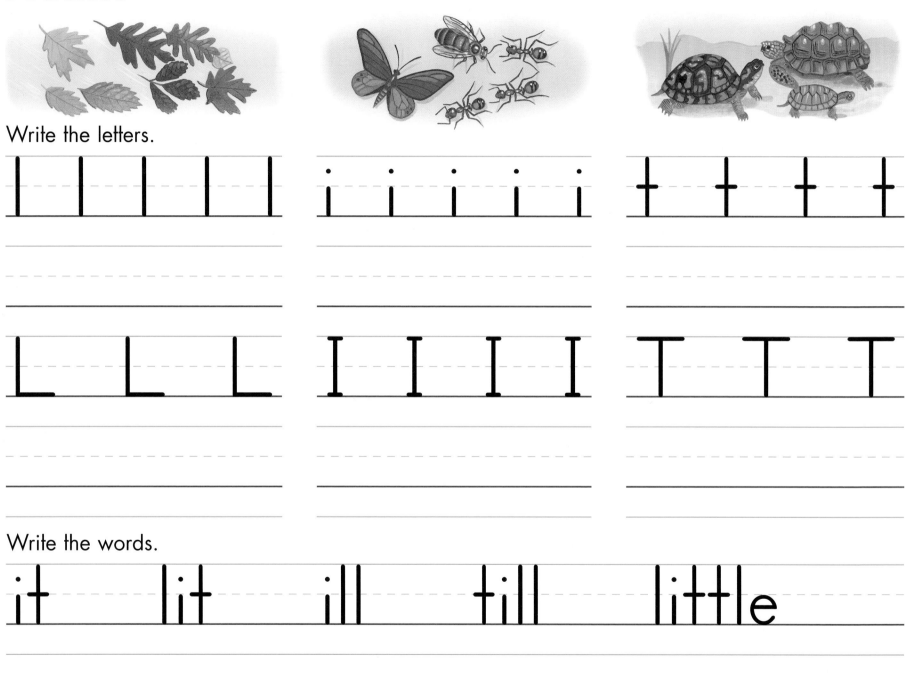

Write the letters.

l l l l l i i i i i t t t t t

L L L I I I I T T T

Write the words.

it lit ill till little

Look at me!

Today is my birthday.

I am one year older.

My Words

Shape

Circle a word you wrote
that has good shape.

39

Name:

Trace and write.

o o o o o

✓

✓

otter hop

Trace and write.

O O O O

✓

✓

Opal Ollie

School to Home

Stroke descriptions to guide letter formation at home:
Circle back all the way around.

o

Circle back all the way around.

O

Write the words.

octopus   off   on   odd

Write the sentence.

Our class took a trip.

On Your Own Write words to finish the sentence.

Our trip was

Name:

Trace and write.

a a a a a

alligator   act

Trace and write.

A A A

Ali Anna

Stroke descriptions to guide letter formation at home:

Circle back all the way around;
push up straight. Pull down straight.

 Slant left. Lift. Slant right. Lift. Slide right.

Write the words.

ant   animal   ask   all

Write the sentence.

All my friends play ball.

On Your Own Write words to finish the sentence.

I can play

Shape

Circle your best letter
that has a / line.

43

Trace and write.

d

Trace and write.

D

duck   dig

Deb   Dan

Stroke descriptions to guide letter formation at home:

d Circle back all the way around; push up straight. Pull down straight.

D Pull down straight. Lift. Slide right; curve forward; slide left.

School to Home

Write the words.

dad   doll   dive   do

Write the sentence.

Do you like dinosaurs?

Write words to finish the sentence.

Dinosaurs are

Shape

Circle your best letter
that has a ◯ line.

45

Practice

Write the letters.

o o o o   a a a a   d d d d

O O O   A A A   D D D

Write the words.

add   odd   dad   dot

Application Write the naming words.

dog

toad

Dan

apple

yard

Amy

My Words

Shape

Circle a word you wrote that has good shape.

47

Trace and write.

? ? ? ? ?

Trace and write.

! ! ! ! ! !

Who? Why?

Good! Wow!

Stroke descriptions to guide formation at home:

? Curve forward; pull down straight.
Lift. Dot.

! Pull down straight.
Lift. Dot.

Write the sentences.

Can you come over?

I will see you soon!

On Your Own Write words to finish the sentence.

I like to see

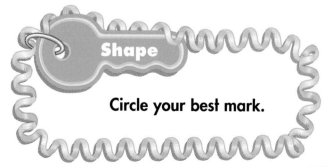

Circle your best mark.

49

Keys to Legibility

Make your writing easy to read.
Look at the size of each letter.

These letters are just the right size.

Writing is fun!

This writing is easy to read.

Tall Letters

Tall letters touch the headline.

K b d

Short Letters

Short letters touch the midline.

o m e

Letters That Go Below the Baseline

Some letters go below the baseline.

j g y

Trace and write tall letters.

T O A L D l t d

Trace and write short letters.

a o c i e v r n

Trace and write letters that go below the baseline.

g p j q y

Name: _____

Trace and write.

 C C C C C

cap   carry

Trace and write.

C C C C

Carlos Cora

School to Home

Stroke descriptions to guide letter formation at home:
Circle back.

C

 Circle back.

52

Write the words.

coat　　car　　cook　　cut

Write the sentence.

Can you count to 20?

On Your Own Write words that begin with **c** or **C**.

Size

Circle your best short letter.

Trace and write.

e e e e e

elephant eat

Trace and write.

E E E E

Ellen Ed

School to Home

Stroke descriptions to guide letter formation at home:
Slide right. Circle back.

e

E Pull down straight. Lift. Slide right. Lift. Slide right; stop short. Lift. Slide right.

Write the words.

egg   end   empty   exit

Write the sentence.

Everyone enjoys stories.

On Your Own Write words that have **e** or **E** in them.

Size

Circle your best letter that goes below the baseline.

Name: _____

Trace and write.

f   f   f   f

fish   find

Trace and write.

F   F   F   F

Fred   Flora

Stroke descriptions to guide letter formation at home:

f   Curve back; pull down straight.
Lift. Slide right.

Pull down straight. Lift. Slide right. Lift.
Slide right; stop short.

Write the words.

fun   family   fall   fly

Write the sentence.

Friends have lots of fun.

On Your Own Write number words that begin with **f** or **F**.

Size

Circle your best tall letter.

Practice

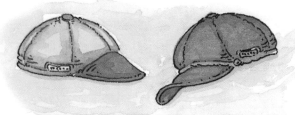  

Write the letters.

c   c   c   c   e   e   e   e   f   f   f   f

C   C   C   E   E   E   F   F   F

Write the words.

face   feet   ice   life

Application   Write the action words.

eat

fill

catch

feed

call

color

My Words

59

Trace and write.

g g g g g

goat   go

Trace and write.

G G G G

Gail   Glen

School to Home

Stroke descriptions to guide letter formation at home:

g Circle back all the way around; push up straight. Pull down straight; curve back.

G Circle back. Slide left.

Write the words.

girl   gate   goes   got

Write the sentence.

Get ready, get set, giggle!

On Your Own Write words that begin with **g** or **G**.

Trace and write.

j   j   j   j   j

✓

✓

jacks jump

Trace and write.

J   J   J   J

✓

✓

Juan Jen

Stroke descriptions to guide letter formation at home:

Pull down straight;
curve back. Lift. Dot.

Pull down straight;
curve back. Lift. Slide right.

62

Write the words.

jam   jar   joke   jog

Write the sentence.

Join our jumping game.

On Your Own   Write words that begin with **j** or **J**.

Size

Circle your best short letter.

Name:

Trace and write.

q   q   q   q

Trace and write.

Q   Q   Q

quilt   quit

Quita Quinn

School to Home

Stroke descriptions to guide letter formation at home:

q Circle back all the way around; push up straight. Pull down straight; curve forward.

Q Circle back all the way around. Lift. Slant right.

64

Write the words.

queen   quart   quarter

Write the sentences.

Quick! It's time to go.

Write words that begin with **qu** or **Qu**.

Size

Circle your best tall letter.

Practice

  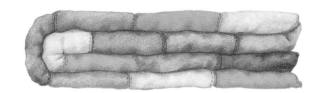

Write the letters.

g g g g g j j j j j q q q q q

G G G J J J Q Q Q

Write the words.

cage jeans grass quite

Application

Write the describing words.

juicy

green

good

jolly

quiet

quick

My Words

Size

Circle a word you wrote that has good size.

Keys to Legibility

Make your writing easy to read.
Look at the spacing between letters.

  **Spacing**

 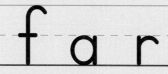 

These letters are too close.	These letters are too far apart.	These letters have good spacing.
close	f a r	good

Circle two words with good spacing between letters.

boy   brother   sister   girl

Trace and write words. Use good spacing between letters.

aunts   uncles   cousins

Make your writing easy to read.
Look at the spacing between words.

These words have good spacing.

This is just right.

There is a finger space between words.

Write a ✔ next to the sentence that has good spacing between words.

This is easy to read.

This is hard to read.

Write the sentence. Use good spacing between words.

I can read this.

Trace and write.

u   u   u   u   u

umbrella

Trace and write.

U   U   U   U   U

Uri   Uma

Stroke descriptions to guide letter formation at home:

Pull down straight;
curve forward; push up.
Pull down straight.

Pull down straight;
curve forward; push up.

70

Write the words.

uncle   us   under   up

Write the sentence.

Use your umbrella now.

On Your Own Tell what you use when it rains.

Spacing

Circle two letters with
good spacing between them.

s

S

Trace and write.

s s s s s

star see

Trace and write.

S S S S S

Sara Seth

School to Home

Stroke descriptions to guide letter formation at home:

s Curve back;
curve forward.

S Curve back;
curve forward.

Write the words.

seal   sun   sit   sell

Write the sentence.

Should I sing a song?

Write the name of a song you like to sing.

Spacing

Circle two words with good spacing between them.

Name:

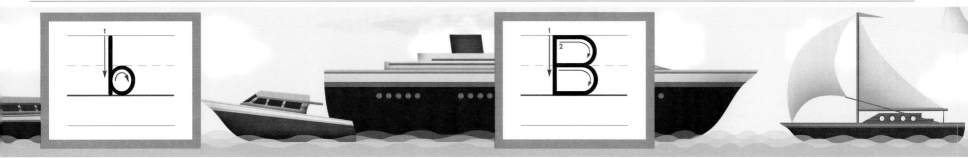

Trace and write.

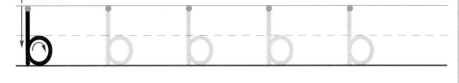

Trace and write.

boat   build

Bill   Beth

School to Home

Stroke descriptions to guide letter formation at home:

Pull down straight;
push up. Circle forward.

Pull down straight. Lift. Slide right;
curve forward; slide left. Slide right;
curve forward; slide left.

Write the words.

bell   baby   bake   bring

Write the sentence.

Big books are great!

On Your Own Tell what kind of books you like.

Spacing

Circle two letters with good spacing between them.

Trace and write.

p p p p p

✓

✓

paint pull

Trace and write.

P P P P

✓

✓

Pat Pedro

Stroke descriptions to guide letter formation at home:

p Pull down straight.
   Push up. Circle forward
   all the way around.

P Pull down straight. Lift.
   Slide right; curve forward;
   slide left.

Write the words.

pen   pig   push   put

Write the sentence.

Please pass the paper.

On Your Own Write a sentence that begins with **Please**.

Spacing

Circle two words with good spacing between them.

Practice

Write the letters.

u u u   s s s   b b b   p p p

U U   S S   B B   P P

Write the words.

bus   pup   cub   cup

Bob bakes bread.

Paula pets a pink pig.

Six snakes have snacks.

My Words

Spacing

Circle a word you wrote
that has good spacing.

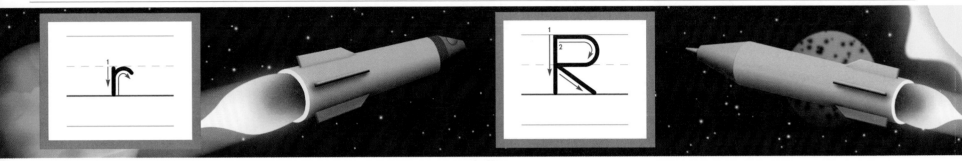

Trace and write.

rocket   run

Trace and write.

Ron   Rosa

School to Home

Stroke descriptions to guide letter formation at home:

r Pull down straight.
Push up; curve forward.

R Pull down straight. Lift.
Slide right; curve forward; slide left.
Slant right.

80

Write the words.

rock   rain   read   ring

Write the sentence.

Read me a story.

On Your Own Tell who reads to you.

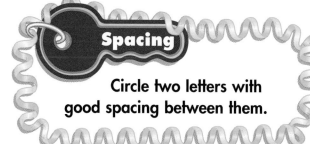

Spacing

Circle two letters with
good spacing between them.

Name: _____

Trace and write.

n

n n n n n

✓

✓

nest   need

Trace and write.

N

N N N N N

✓

✓

Nina   Nicky

Stroke descriptions to guide letter formation at home:

n   Pull down straight. Push up;
curve forward; pull down straight.

   Pull down straight. Lift. Slant right. Push up straight.

82

Write the words.

nine   nail   nap   nod

Write the sentences.

No napping! Wake up!

On Your Own Tell at what time you wake up.

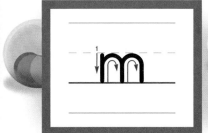 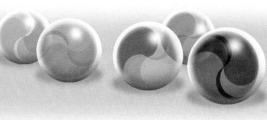 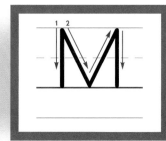 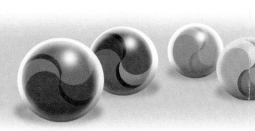

Trace and write.

 m m m m

✓

✓

marble meet

Trace and write.

M M M M

✓

✓

Matt Ming

 **Stroke descriptions to guide letter formation at home:**

m Pull down straight. Push up; curve forward;
pull down straight. Push up; curve forward;
pull down straight.

 M Pull down straight. Lift. Slant right.
Slant up. Pull down straight.

Write the words.

mom   moon   mail   miss

Write the sentence.

My lunch is yummy!

On Your Own Tell what you like for lunch.

Spacing

Circle two letters with
good spacing between them.

Name:

Trace and write.

h h h h h

horse hug

Trace and write.

H H H H

Holly Hank

School to Home

Stroke descriptions to guide letter formation at home:

Pull down straight. Push up;
curve forward; pull down straight.

Pull down straight. Lift.
Pull down straight. Lift. Slide right.

86

Write the words.

hill house have hop

Write the sentence.

How can I help you?

On Your Own Tell how you help others.

Spacing

Circle two words with good spacing between them.

Practice

Write the letters.

r r r   n n n   m m m   h h h

R R   N N   M M   H H

Write the words.

name   room   home   horn

Application   Write the list of things to do.

1. Return Nate's hat.

2. Make a map.

3. Have a snack.

Spacing

Circle a word you wrote
that has good spacing.

Keys to Legibility

Make your writing easy to read.
Look at the slant of the letters.

Slant

This writing is easy to read.

This writing is straight up and down.

Hello, everyone!

These letters are straight up and down.

straight

Circle each word that is straight up and down.

smile   smile   *smile*   *smile*

laugh   laugh   laugh   laugh

Trace and write words. Make the letters straight up and down.

giggle   sing   dance

hum   play

Name:

Trace and write.

V V V V V

Trace and write.

V V V V

van   vote

Vic   Viv

Stroke descriptions to guide letter formation at home:

Slant right.
Slant up.

Slant right.
Slant up.

Write the words.

vest   video   visit   very

Write the sentence.

Vera loves vegetables.

On Your Own   Tell what you love to eat.

Slant

Circle a letter that is straight up and down.

Trace and write.

y Y Y Y Y

yo-yo yawn

Trace and write.

Y Y Y Y Y

Yoko Yoshi

Stroke descriptions to guide letter formation at home:

School to Home

Slant right.
Lift. Slant left.

Slant right.
Lift. Slant left.
Pull down straight.

Write the words.

yard   you   yell   yes

Write the sentence.

You can play with me.

Tell what games you like to play.

Slant

Circle a word that is
straight up and down.

Name: _____

Trace and write.

Trace and write.

✓

✓

✓

✓

wagon wait

Will Wendy

School to Home

Stroke descriptions to guide letter formation at home:

Slant right. Slant up.
Slant right. Slant up.

Slant right. Slant up.
Slant right. Slant up.

Write the words.

winter   wall   want   wish

Write the sentence.

Will it snow today?

On Your Own Tell what your weather is like today.

Slant

Circle a letter that is straight up and down.

Practice

Write the letters.

v v v y y y w w w

V V V Y Y Y W W

Write the words.

your wave vet way

Application   Write an invitation.

You're Invited!

When: Friday 4:00

Where: Valley School

What: a party

Slant

Circle a word you wrote
that has good slant.

Name: _____

Trace and write.

x X X X X

fox mix

Trace and write.

X X X X

Xena Xavier

Stroke descriptions to guide letter formation at home:

x Slant right.
Lift. Slant left.

X Slant right.
Lift. Slant left.

Write the words.

box   six   taxi   fix

Write the sentence.

X marks the spot.

On Your Own Tell where you would hide a treasure.

Slant

Circle a word that is
straight up and down.

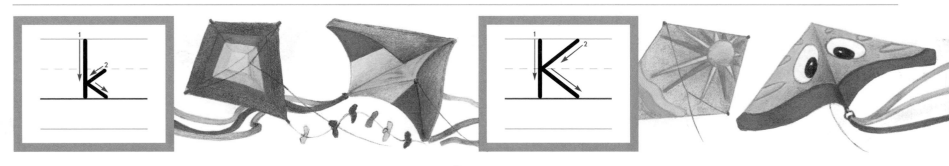

Trace and write.

k k k k k

Trace and write.

K K K K K

kite   keep

Ken   Kisha

Stroke descriptions to guide letter formation at home:

k Pull down straight.
Lift. Slant left. Slant right.

  Pull down straight.
Lift. Slant left. Slant right.

Write the words.

kids   keys   kick   kiss

Write the sentence.

Kids like to fly kites.

On Your Own   Tell what other things kids like to do.

Slant

Circle a letter that is straight up and down.

Name: _____

Trace and write.

z z z z z z

✓

✓

zebra zip

Trace and write.

Z Z Z Z

✓

✓

Zoey Zach

Stroke descriptions to guide letter formation at home:

z Slide right.
Slant left. Slide right.

Z Slide right.
Slant left. Slide right.

Write the words.

zoo fuzzy maze zoom

Write the sentence.

Z is a zigzag letter.

On Your Own Name things that zigzag.

Slant

Circle a word that is
straight up and down.

Practice

Write the letters.

x x x x x   k k k k   z z z z

X X X   K K K   Z Z Z

Write the words.

buzz zero next king

Application   Write the story of the Gingerbread Man.

Mix the batter.

Bake the cookie.

It zooms away.

My Words

Circle a word you wrote
that has good slant.

Number Words Write the numerals and the number words.

1 one uno   2 two dos

3 three tres   4 four cuatro

5 five cinco

On Your Own Write the Spanish words for **3** and **4**.

Write the numerals and the number words.

6 six   seis   7 seven   siete

8 eight ocho   9 nine nueve

10 ten   diez

On Your Own Write a numeral and a number word
to tell your age.

Shape

Circle a word you wrote
that has good shape.

109

Days of the Week

Write the name of each day.

Monday   Tuesday

Wednesday   Thursday

Friday   Saturday   Sunday

Dear _____ ,

Today is _____

_____

_____

_____

Your friend, _____

_____

Size

Circle a word you wrote that has good size.

Months   Write the name of each month.

January   February

March   April   May

June   July   August

112

September   October

November   December

On Your Own Write the name of two holiday months.

Spacing

Circle a word you
wrote that has good spacing.

Writing Quickly

Make your writing easy to read.
Write this rhyme.

Rain, rain, go away.

Come again another day.

Now write it again.
Try to write faster.

Record of Student's Handwriting Skills

Manuscript

	Needs Improvement	Shows Mastery		Needs Improvement	Shows Mastery
Uses good sitting position	☐	☐	Writes **e** and **E**	☐	☐
Positions paper correctly	☐	☐	Writes **f** and **F**	☐	☐
Holds pencil correctly	☐	☐	Writes **g** and **G**	☐	☐
Writes vertical lines	☐	☐	Writes **j** and **J**	☐	☐
Writes horizontal lines	☐	☐	Writes **q** and **Q**	☐	☐
Writes backward circle lines	☐	☐	Writes **u** and **U**	☐	☐
Writes forward circle lines	☐	☐	Writes **s** and **S**	☐	☐
Writes slant lines	☐	☐	Writes **b** and **B**	☐	☐
Writes numerals **1–5**	☐	☐	Writes **p** and **P**	☐	☐
Writes numerals **6–10**	☐	☐	Writes **r** and **R**	☐	☐
Writes **l** and **L**	☐	☐	Writes **n** and **N**	☐	☐
Writes **i** and **I**	☐	☐	Writes **m** and **M**	☐	☐
Writes **t** and **T**	☐	☐	Writes **h** and **H**	☐	☐
Writes **o** and **O**	☐	☐	Writes **v** and **V**	☐	☐
Writes **a** and **A**	☐	☐	Writes **y** and **Y**	☐	☐
Writes **d** and **D**	☐	☐	Writes **w** and **W**	☐	☐
Writes a question mark	☐	☐	Writes **x** and **X**	☐	☐
Writes an exclamation point	☐	☐	Writes **k** and **K**	☐	☐
Writes **c** and **C**	☐	☐	Writes **z** and **Z**	☐	☐

Index